MACMILLAN READER
STARTER LEVEL

JONATHAN SWIFT

Gulliver's Travels in Lilliput

Retold by María José Lobo
and Pepita Subirà

macmillan
education

Macmillan Readers is a series of engaging narrative texts designed to stimulate learners while enhancing their language skills, building literacy and boosting reading confidence. Through captivating stories and fascinating cultural themes, learners will explore a diversity of scenarios that foster vocabulary expansion, comprehension skills and a lifelong love of reading.

The right reader at every stage

Tailored to each learner's stage of language proficiency, our six levels feature text adapted to match the skill level. With controlled vocabulary and grammar, learners can read freely and immerse themselves in the story. When more challenging words are introduced, either the text will provide sufficient context to aid understanding or a full explanation will be provided in the Glossary.

Readers for all, anywhere, anytime

Macmillan Readers are perfect for shared, guided and independent reading. Whether in traditional print, immersive audio or the convenient eBook, Macmillan Readers are equally effective for in-class activities, paired discussions or solo reading at home or on the move.

Reading for pleasure, knowledge and well-being

Regular reading and reading for pleasure:

- increases reading confidence, benefiting all literacy skills, not just reading.
- reinforces and enriches vocabulary, providing a variety of contexts.
- expands general knowledge.
- supports concentration, inner reflection and well-being.

Macmillan Readers will inspire a love for reading in English while nurturing essential language skills. Unlock new worlds, expand horizons and embark on an adventure in English!

(NOTE: While the content of Macmillan Readers is evaluated for age suitability, we kindly remind parents and teachers that they are ultimately responsible for determining whether a particular book is appropriate for their child or student.)

sea

storm

wave

ship

beach

bow

arrow

horse

temple

tree

mountain

garden

emperor

officer

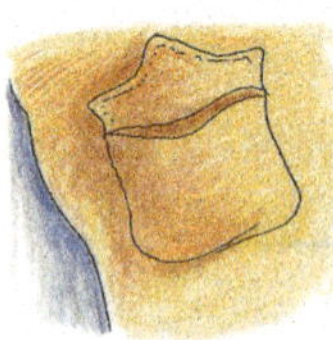

pocket

egg

It is 4th May, 1699. The Antelope is going to the Far East.

One night the sea is rough.

There are a lot of waves. The ship and the other men disappear under the water. Gulliver swims and swims.

Finally, Gulliver arrives at a beach. He cannot see any houses. He is very tired and he goes to sleep.

There is something on Gulliver's hand.
It is moving up his arm.

Gulliver opens his eyes. He sees a very little man.

The man is about 15 centimetres tall. He is looking at Gulliver. Gulliver is very surprised.

Gulliver says 'Hello' to the little man. The little man runs away!

There are hundreds of little men. They have got bows and arrows. They speak a strange language.

Gulliver is very hungry. He is very thirsty too.

But the little men do not understand Gulliver. He moves his hand up and down. Finally, his hand is free. He points to his mouth.

Now the little men understand. They give Gulliver meat, bread, fruit and milk. Gulliver is happy.

Gulliver goes to sleep again. The little men take him to the city. They need more than 1000 horses!

Gulliver wakes up. He is next to a big temple. He cannot escape.

Gulliver stands up. He can see a city, trees and mountains. Everything is very small.

One day the emperor visits Gulliver. He speaks to Gulliver, but Gulliver does not understand the emperor.

The emperor sends ten clever teachers. They teach Gulliver their language. Gulliver learns very quickly. The country's name is Lilliput. The language is called Lilliputian. Gulliver is very happy. Now he can talk to the little people.

One day Gulliver asks the emperor a question.

But the emperor is not sure. 'Is Gulliver dangerous?' he thinks. The emperor asks some officers to look in Gulliver's pockets. Gulliver helps the men. The officers make a list of the things they find.

They tell the emperor what is in Gulliver's pockets.

Gulliver is free now. He visits the city. The children play with him in the streets. Gulliver is very happy.

One day the emperor talks to Gulliver.

Gulliver helps the emperor.
He goes to Blefuscu and pulls its ships to Lilliput.
Now Blefuscu cannot attack Lilliput.

The emperor of Lilliput is very happy. But there are some bad men in Lilliput. They want to kill Gulliver. 'He is too big. He eats too much,' say the bad men.

So one day Gulliver leaves Lilliput. He goes to Blefuscu and looks for new adventures there.

Macmillan Education Limited
4 Crinan Street
London N1 9XW

Companies and representatives throughout the world

Macmillan Readers Starter Level Gulliver's Travels in Lilliput
ISBN: 978-1-035-16081-5
Macmillan Readers Starter Level Gulliver's Travels in Lilliput with eBook and Resources
ISBN: 978-1-035-16084-6

This is a retold version by María José Lobo and Pepita Subirà of the original work by Jonathan Swift.

First published 2008
This edition published 2024

Illustrated by Rowel Boyd Friers MBE
Cover image by Alamy/Pictorial Press

Printed and bound in Brasil
2025
2